I’ve Birthed an Idea of You

S. Bruzon

I’ve Birthed an Idea of You
Copyright © 2023 S. Bruzon
DARK THIRTY POETRY PUBLISHING
ISBN: 978-1-7392546-5-0

Bruzon. S
First edition

Artwork by S. Bruzon

DTPP13

DARK
THIRTY
POETRY
PUBLISHING

For Beli, who taught me how to listen.

Black Hole

stimulate yourself in
the morning
your small frame
expands
into
words
and takes the form
of poetry

wake
to find the bed
wet with gasoline
and urine

every day
fucks you into a stupor
genitals
dire
consequences
stars in the sky
that live in the frizz of your hair

ashes in the spaces
between your fingers
mother's
cigarette
of indifference

blinds
that paint shadows on the wall
blindsided

when somebody
walks back and forth
against the background
of your day

the books that you
should have shoved down your throat
like a crucifix

but you stopped mid-prayer
when you were six

and you never went back to it

Hail Mary,
you'll have sunken into your
most traumatic dream
by thirteen.

Hail Mary,
you'll be on your knees again
when you realize where you've been.

you'll learn to like the swept floors
you'll learn to light your Sunday
candles
and put crosses on your doors

when you cut it out of yourself
like a tumor,
when the vein is ruptured
and you nod
as they tell you

it is over

and you're better
and you're older

in the street
at life's intersection
like an old newspaper
in the attic,

don't you wish
you could speak
about it
honest?

this part
is dark,
darker,
darkest.

it sucks you in
like a black hole.

this kind of frown only exists
on inanimate objects
this kind of disease
only belongs to you.

watch as it grows legs and arms
feel it smother you
in the silence
only you can hear

then walk the way of exile.

you do not belong on the other side
of it

this part is dark,
darker,
darkest.

something so
true
that even
God can't keep you
from it

something so
mute
and dejected
that
even the light
cannot speak out
against it

wake up
wake up
let it enter and leave you

from the gasoline and urine
to the crucifix in your throat,

you find that there
is nothing
beyond it–

you will sink
before you ever learn to float.

The Past and Past It

to hell with the pills
they feed you milk
and forget to pump your stomach

your little sister cries

dangles life before your eyes

you were born too late;
you should have been older.

this was supposed to be the end
but it's beginning again
and colder

hands in the sand
orange juice breath
pulp in between your teeth

you dream,
you dream.

naptime
you don't feel tired
stale animal crackers
xylophone you can't play

they call your parents

you ask to see your friends
they call your parents

what they break
will take you years to mend

and the lines on your palms
are foreign
and they say you'll live very long.

you hope that they're wrong.

A Stuffed Wild Animal

silly silhouette madness
suburban ghost of your dreams
this is not a love poem
this is everything in between.

mailbox white fence carpet burn,
I fall I fall
I'm falling.
off the bed,

wake up on the floor,
my mother thinks I'm dead.

a field of bad reputations,
I've a calling.
it's not beauty,
it's everything else.

but that's how you know it's
really beautiful, anyway.

It's beautiful
that I wrote a piece of this
(a piece of you)
at every stop light today
the traffic was slow
minutes passed.

it’s beautiful that they spit on your
“welcome home” carpet,
but it still feels like home to you,

and I still feel welcomed.

it’s beautiful that
we throw the newspaper on the lawn
and we leave it there

empty out the ash
at the lake
and watch it float away on little boats
made up of wind and longing.

maybe we’ll grow into
some common sense.

maybe we’re worth
a few cents when we’re
together.

maybe you’ll convince me to live
a little longer.

I don’t know.
time seeps slowly
into us
into the holes in our souls
we made to bring us closer.

so undress me now,
do good in doing bad,

sort out my messy drawers
and crooked expressions,

set fire to that lawn,
or else choke on the
flame.

What I'm trying to say
is that our knees
were not made for floors,

and our bodies are never bodies
but doors.

And it's beautiful
that this is not
something that happens every day,
it's not the newspaper
not the carpet
not the traffic delay.

It's the rush in your veins
and the rush that you are,
all things untouched and unforeseen.

but this is not a love poem.

this is everything
in between.

Indefinite Spaces

Tolerance fails me again.
noise cancellation for the silence
yellow light for the kitchen
instead of white.

And a reflection on the stove,
a gas leak,
something that should've
been shut off
but never was.

(Indefinite)

I find gaps in the places
I forgot existed on my body,
like small voids
spread out over my skin.

I say,
we like to live in segments,
we like to say nothing ever happened
until we are sure
 nothing ever did.

Except we feel it breathe down our backs,
like the stranger who stares at you
for too long at the grocery store,
or the car that turns too close to yours

while you’re at a red light.

(Indefinite)

What are we missing?

What is this absence you speak of?

I think I’d like to wake
to no ceiling above my head,

to the sky there
waiting for me
instead.

And I’d like to cry about it:
that lack thereof,
that longing for.

I’d like to penetrate through every wall
of my life
and sink so desperate,
that we are inseparable,
my life and I

(Indefinite).

She's Leaving Home

folk music,
a few skirts.

more dreams
than nightmares,

more to life than what hurts.

and my favorite guitar,
and a copy of the novel
that made me
feel again,
that carried me
this far:

The Waves.

the waves
carry me again,
as far as they can,

they said they'll let me know if I've
become too heavy to hold on to.

I know my legs are longer now,
but I'm just as blue,

though it's true:

I can't tell a lie,
I'm a few years older,
and I don't have one heart,

I have two.

so worry not.

I'm on my way to give this one away,
but this other one's for you.

so worry not.
let's untangle that knot
in my hair,

I demand nothing but dreams
from now on.

to uncover that same childhood fever
hidden underneath everything we love
and everything we are.

to uncover the home
we learned the twenty-six letters of the alphabet in,

the way our love smells
when I walk into it
and walk around it,

close my eyes,

to see everyone that surrounds
me.

and I them.

one thing bleeding into another,
my existence preceded by my lover's,
my hair being nothing like my mother's,

feeling good for myself,
taking the books off the shelves,

boxes for my books,
boxes for my life,
my life into boxes.

squeeze you into my morning
before I go,
when I'll be back,
I don't know.
I don't know.

all my cards say
I'm leaving home.

and they're never wrong.

I'll be gone,
soon,
I'll be gone.

folk music, a few skirts.
my own hand on my knee.

there is more to life than what hurts,
and it waits
somewhere
for me.

Portrait of Myself as a Vessel for Freudian Desires

I've seen three psychics since I let the idea of
us go,

and a psychiatrist who flirted with me
because he was your age,

so he figured he had a chance

because I'm fragmented,
so this is romance.

this is romance:

masculine projections
that are never enough.

old hands,
lonely in their longing,
soft in the places
where they're rough.

years worth of fear,
never found the one,
so it must be me.

why must my womb be a refuge

for men without mothers?

why must my breasts be your airbags,
and my long, black hair the covers
you hide underneath

until it's safe enough for you to
act like a man.

why must my womb be a refuge
for men without mothers?

why must you crawl back into my mind
to steal another phrase out of my mouth
to tuck away into the waistband
of all your wasted time.

my ribbons are torn;
I'm no good.

I'm not an artist like you thought.
I'm not misunderstood.

I'm soft flesh
over ligaments,
and I've got a case of
old matriarchy blues:

I'm not the mother life gives you,
I'm the mother that you choose.

I’m not an artist.

I’m someone who knows how to love,

someone who loves
to lose.

someone who loves
in order to lose

who loses

in order
to love.

so,

take my ribbons,
pink organs
in your ripe
and useful hands.

I’ll ask you to feed me,
and tie the ribbons back when it’s time.

but I’ll never know what I want to eat,
(too busy spoon-feeding you attention
to pay any
to my own hunger)

and I won't ask you to have patience
for the woman that you need
but don't love.

and I'll love you,
I'll love you,

and you'll love me,
you'll convince yourself
that you really do

because my soul is
so contagious, so profound
that it's outrageous,

that it gives the impression
that the receiver has it, too.

but I am only the vessel, the surrogate
for the mother who could not
love you.

Waiting Room Anagrams

Waiting room cubicle,
rows and rows of washed-out
white tiles.
Anything but pure,
everything but pure.

"It's
        A
          Girl."

Blood on the tip of the finger,
reels of it linger,
reels of my design,

like your body
reclined on the seat,
your spine protruding
through your back.

Myself
on your lap.
Someone
up there
watches.

Your shadow looks
as if it were watercolor
on those walls,

and when one of us rises,
one of them falls.

I like being reduced to a thing
you can hit
or caress
or kiss
or destroy.

Waiting room cubicle,
reels and reels of mourning.

“Are you sure you want it

                    removed?”

      I’m sure.

My womb has food poisoning.
It has eaten me whole.
It will eat me for the rest of my life.

It kicks me out at 18,
it speaks to me behind
a closed door,

it calls me Madonna,
it calls me the whore,

it laughs at me,
when I beg for more.

But who am I, if I am not yours?

Waiting room cubicle.
Rows and rows of hollow wombs.

Bodily fluids on the floors,
my frail body next to yours,
in utero and outside of it,

Who am I, if I am not yours?

I flip through the pages,
lick the blood off my fingers.
It'll only last a moment.
It won't burn forever.

A paper cut is not your mother.

Desire is not your owner.

These people don't exist.

You're just young and want to be kissed.

These people don't exist.

And it's not getting removed—you're just not on that list.

Addictions and Things

your therapist told you
to quit it
as if it were cigarettes

panties
doused in sweat
and spit

a stranger on your lawn
cutting the grass for you

the party that left you blue
that you could have enjoyed
but you can't stop yourself

you always have to split,

and you can't quit
and you can't quit
and you can't.

dances in your yard,
things to do before
life gets hard
again.

choosing to not choose
anything.

choosing to choose you
again
again
again.

peonies at your window
that grow from the walls,

the sprinklers
like waterfalls,

cars rush by
like people have somewhere to be
when they know
that no one has anywhere

they need to go.

everything can be
beautiful.

don't you want beautiful things?

But it's not a cigarette.

forget the poison of it,
patch it up with plaster

it's not a cigarette,

it's not a cigarette.

It'll kill us faster.

The Disappearing Act

you're asking
(pleading)
show me where the light is.

unrepentant,
I ask you to undress me.

you are a nonconformist
that has tried to conform–

you strip me from behind
and try to wear me
like a uniform.

I,
too,
have tried to
wear you.

I,
too,
have mistaken
sin
for
an excuse
to excavate

the
carcass
within,

the swan's
frail body
that has since rot.

the smell
of it that fills us up
until
the ashes come
out of our mouths
every time we speak
recite
sing
or fuck.

you're asking
(pleading)
would you mix your ashes
in with mine?

yes

and I can be the urn

until it is your turn

to be mine.

to unspeak
to unlove
to undo
to be penetrated

in the

aperture
that most defines you.

dressed in white,
I could be a puritan,
or what's left of Him–

a skeleton
a handmaid.

and
yes, I am handmade.

only under your hand
am I real.

when the time comes,

forget the ashes.

like them,
we want to disappear.

if you want to be unseen,

don't worry don't touch me

I,
too,
am not here.

Observations of Loss

I cling faithfully to any
instance of you:

my time at the cemetery,
a table for two
in the back of that place

where I have laid down to die
more than once or twice
already.

Now I hang like a light
off that ceiling.

I gave up the dream long ago,

like I bought it from you,
and it didn't fit me.

So allow me to feel what it feels like
to be a foot in your shoe,
a moment in your mind,

a feeling of yours
with no translation.

let me feel what is feels like
to be the stranger

that sits next to you
at the station,

the last bite of your dinner
or breakfast
or lunch.

That poem I'm sure you
wrote and then threw into the fire.

Let me feel what it feels like
to be the woman in your bed,

No longer lost,
no longer mine
or yours,

just a simple observation.

For it is April,
meet me at the station,

I think I must
lie down to die
again.

My Room in Bordeaux

I shut my blinds.
Violently, silently
I slip into the softness
of my room in Bordeaux.

Really, France sounds like you.
I guessed it all along.

Your laughter rings through
these streets,
or maybe it's only the violinist I met
who's more of a vagabond
than anything else,
as you never really know where
you'll meet him,

or who you'll meet when you do.

I still think it sounds like you.

The silky sunsets
that the sky
drapes over this city, like curtains,
remind me of your gentle touch,
never a lover's but almost as much.

I thought I'd be here with you,
but I thought a lot of things —

none of them ever came true.

When I speak in the tongue,
it feels raw to the ear,
as if it's only natural
that I be fluent in what I fear.
and what I fear is myself mostly,
and that I may never have you.

Bordeaux rocks me to sleep now,
I slip further now,

My blinds are fully-closed now,
but my heart is open.

I have coffee every morning
at an antique café,
and it means nothing,
but I long for it all the time.

I walk around in the rain
and sing Véronique Sanson.
My mind goes to somewhere in The States,
where you are,
at least twice every day.

This is my life
that I thought would be ours.

France sounds like you.

And really, I guessed it would.

The violinist friend of mine,
whom I never speak to but understand
through soul-searching silence,
tells me that he plays to remind me of you.

Or perhaps I make you up as I go—
as I slip into the softness of my room
in Bordeaux.

Hung Up

Simplicity, take me back.
towel on a silver rack,
tiles on the walls and floors,
and you are on your back.

The cornea,
the pupil,
the iris,
private lenses
of the body,

come down
and hold us
so that we may know
the people
we will never be,

the people

we will forget
to meet.

And it comes down,
it rains down on me:

Newspaper clippings
of my face
in your dreams,

celluloid fever
of when I was sixteen
and meant to say something
but didn't.

You are a man.

I am scarcely a woman.

And we are no poets.

Soldier-on, up, home,
save yourself for when you get there.

Put the tears in the glove compartment.

You know that I do.

You are not the stranger
that you tell yourself you are.

Towel on a silver rack.
I keep poems in my pocket
that might never leave me
but that you know
like you know your mother's love,

maddening and relentless,

I am.

I keep poems in my pocket.
A penny somewhere
in that expressionless catastrophe
for every time
I thought you might be mine
and that thought turned and drowned.

You are no better than
the ceiling I pray to.

Towel on a silver rack,
I'm longing,
simplicity, take me back.

I am

extremist ideations,
I am bloody, womanly cessations,
stares that could cut you open
and make you lose everything you have
ever held onto.

Isn't it exciting,
this prospect of dying?

and nostalgia.

and teenage yearning.

What have you learned?

Unlearning.

Like I have to recite
the lines you've written
backwards,
like I need to catch your face
and record it,
hold it,
own it.

Like I am no poet,
but I will make use of it
until you are nothing,
as you once were.

Until it is so delicately
black

that even ourselves we cannot unpack.

Nothing. Nothing. Nothing.
Until it is a towel
on a silver rack.

Womanhood, Poverty, and Love

Silk sheets to cover suburban disaster
and holes on the mattress we bought for ten cents,
at first it was you that made me love it.

Now it's only routine.
Your face under the tainted dining room lights.
Your heart laid bare on the dinner table.
And you call it womanhood.

Womanhood consists of sacrifice, you say.
I have nothing, but I give everything, you say.

It's true.
My first lesson was how to be like you.
The teacher was myself.

I failed,
lost my cents all over the country.

We almost sat at the table together,
until a taxi driver called to tell you I left one,
the bartender two,
the bicyclist three,

And the man in the suede suit said I left four
before I recognized his voice
and hung up the phone.

The cents were gone,
but we had the money for our silk sheets,
so you promised you weren't mad at me.

When the millions of people
in and out of the door,
from the morning to the night,
came by,
I began to pretend,
since I couldn't find another way.

It was easy to lie to others:
cross my legs,
paint my lips,
curl my hair,
remove all signs of nature
like a disease.

then I started to see the cracks
in your womanhood
and realized you only pretended, too.

Neither of us knew.

Now, I have a secret:
the silk sheets mean nothing to me,
but I wrap myself in them every night
because you say they are important.

And I made a hole in my pocket

because I didn’t care about the money.

And I love you,
because underneath the layers of false
womanhood you put on for everyone but me,
underneath the years of mourning only I can see,
you are yourself.

Your tears in my coffee cup,
The way you dance after you work yourself to death,
You’ve got the spirit of extravagance
that longs to escape.

Despite the poverty,
In the river of our love
And faces revealed behind closed doors,
we are free.

Analogy Using Film

dark negatives coming
from the darkroom
overexposed myself to you

man is a thief
with no reason.

what makes you sad,
man says,
is the season.

and yet the shutter of the soul
only knows click
click

shoot.

chase the train down
until God smells the torment

from the sweat in your forehead
to the knot in your stomach
that man explains is love.

and God pulls the emergency brakes.

click
click

shoot.

the people you wanted
rush out of the train.
the panic
when it comes to an end
reminds you of being born
again.

and his face flashes against
your own
and
there's a click
and a shoot

but no image.

it might exist
and you'll never know what it is

you'll never be able to prove
that it happened.

hike up your dress
and ruin the last minute
you have with it

gather everything you love
like flowers you have picked
from the ground

sell your material belongings
bury the rest
it doesn't belong to you

this earth was made to nurture
what you were made to kill

be harsher with your apologies
forgive yourself for never forgiving
them
for never forgiving you

do not pretend that you don't know
that everything will die when you do

someone else will leave behind
what you failed to find

and the rest will come up
in dark negatives from
the darkroom.

The Kiss Was An Accident. I Meant To Punch You In The Mouth Instead

1.

Kissing the magnets
Before I put them on the fridge
Reminds me of the time
We fell against the tree,
Speaking to ghosts
Like they are friends,
You put a bandaid on my knee–

I kiss your face before I leave.
Eyes, nose, cheeks, lips,
The black lcd font number ticks over our heads,
Time, time, time,
Loose threads.

I wish I never found out.

2.

What have we lost?
What have we gained?

Don't refrain
If I call out your name,
And you want to reach out.

Do it.

If you reach out long enough,
I might reach back,

Except you know that I'm through with it,

My hand unreachable,
Severed from my body,
Something else to surrender to you,

I'm through.

I don't want to reach out my hand,
I don't want to hold yours.

I won't give you the satisfactions,
I won't give you the cures,
For I don't have any yet,

And pinning magnets on the fridge
Feels wrong
When it is you I want to pin on the fridge.
Or the image I had of you,
Purified, romanticized,

Causing me to be
Vilified, cast aside,
Told that those twelve years of my life
Were a lie.

Stay a little longer.
Your wings taped on a page in my scrapbook—
A distant memory,
A way to say that I took something, too.

Who are you?
I've never met you before.

Your reflection
On the microwave,
Your hand on the stove,
Fluorescent orange
And yellow
And blue.

Who are you?
I've never met you before.

The tv is on,
and it hasn't rained like this
Since we were three.
I think about the tree.
The magnets piled up,
You said you loved me.

And I keep driving past the
Places I was last,
Looking for myself
Like looking for old covers,
Like looking for car keys,
Like looking for past lovers.

I end up at your house,
In your mother's bedroom,
Listening to the same sounds of nothingness
I lost my childhood to.

I need our old covers
To hide underneath.

I don't know how to grieve, ok?

I don't know how to grieve.

3.

Kissing your face before I leave.

Newborn

with a
gut full of greed
upon arrival,

if money's what we need,
we're lost.

as lost as your natal
moment,
as lost as your face
under sterile white.

I know that light feels harsh
against your newly found eyes.

I know you have no idea
what they will make you do
when you land
when you land
when you land.

I reach for your small hand

most things take longer
longer
than planned.

so come again,
take off your disguise

come to me

shameless

come to me
nameless,

already baptized
in the church of your
body.

and face forward.

they will
fill your head with water

until you are top-full
like a tank
and there are fish in your brain
that swim
up to the surface of you

and take a breath to feel
how we feel
to feel how we feel
to feel how we feel

and how is that?

with a gut full of greed
upon arrival,
you feel what I feel
you feel what I feel
you feel what I feel

everything is born
in the same way which
it dies.

tears fill
your newborn eyes.

The Last Poem I'll Write for You

I picked you up carefully,
the way a child does with
an insect.

I kissed you,
(though I'm not sure I was supposed to)

because I was desperate and curious.

I wanted to see that what would happen
if I gave myself away to something
other than
the words,

which are sometimes everything

and other times
nothing.

I wanted to give of myself

the way I've seen the flowers give to
the seasons:

both by dying
and
by living.

I know you now,
inside and out;

though I don't know if you know me.

I've lived and died about you.

I've seen you in my dreams.

I've slept in your bed,
I've slept in your body.

I've birthed an idea of you
that you could be happy with
so I could excuse myself

for loving you madly,

even when you could not love me.

yes,
I've been your lover,

as I have been your friend.

I've been the pitstop
of all your traveler dreams,

somewhere to rest your head.

so, I am your bitch,
it's among
the things I am:

woman,
lover,

sacrificial
lamb.

Vows

For B

this is the part where the mystique dries up
and turns to mold.

this is the part where furniture imprints
on naked skin,
and shoes are put to dry
in the sun.

where it matters not
that something is happy,
where it matters only
that it is alive.

this is the nonsensical
chapter,
the
"I want to write happier"
the skin
to the tumor
to the body
that is blue.

you dig my illness
a grave to lie in;
I keep its death
close to my chest:
a vow of gratefulness
to you.

a single vow of

I do,
I do give it
now
instead of take it.

and then I lie about it
when it becomes exposed again
and let my bare legs
swing back and forth
over it,

lest I take myself
into that winter
I know that I will
never come back from.

and you might say something like
"But you love Billie Holiday!"
and I'll say
that jazz makes me
wish I could scream louder than I do.

something about the color blue again
something like
I'm almost almost
almost
blue.

and you,
you might say
"this is the only life in which you have
come out of the other end alive,
alive

and on fire”

and I might say
this is the only life,
there is no other.
then make a vow to the end,

a vow that won’t end.

and you might say
beautiful things,
and I might say ugly ones,

and we might live
to say them both

again
and again.

America and Elsewhere

I’ve had beautiful
Cars of luxury,
mornings wrapped in silk,
a kiss on the lips,
a jar full of milk.

I’ve had beauty
my entire life.
Now give me ugly.
Give me horrific:
Rust on rails,
spit on sidewalks,
dirt under fingernails.

I want to see desperation,
sweat and torn skin,
conditioned as a first-class citizen
in a country of first-class citizens.

(Aren’t we so very lucky?)

Don’t give me the same half-truths
I've grown accustomed to.
I need new,
need to see you beg me
to stay a little longer
for coffee in your broken rocking chair

Because you’re lonely.
And time is nothing—
and love is everything.

I'll sit on your lap,
call myself a visitor of your land,
when god knows I belong here,

if only you'll tear my dress,
allow me to breathe again.
I'm exhausted of the lace, too,
that stained fabric that covers my face.
My wedding dress is disgrace,
and I wear it with gladness.

I've married a life of nothing
and mistaken it for everything.

So let's play The Beatles
in the kitchen
like we used to do.
I'll tell you I'll stay for coffee,
when really, I mean to say I'll stay for you.

Show me the mirror
in your room,
the one in the dark,
and let me be naked
in the silence between us
that is so thick it feels like clothing.

Let me kiss you,
and then forget to pull away.
You aren't beautiful—
beauty means nothing anyway.

You aren't beautiful,
beauty means nothing
anyway.

On Salvation

on the rejection of anything
and everything
like asphalt and concrete
over dreams.

paradise is another word
for unsatisfied,
for wanting something
on the other side of
your life.

we say each other's names
in vain,
shout until there's blood
coming from the sky
instead of rain.

we grow tired of the prettiness of things.

we see the truth
more often,
not only
when it is appropriate:

lovers make mistakes.
feeling is reduced to an impulse.
what we say is complicated
is always simple.

family is a concept.
people are not real.

put it all in your arms.
borrow it when you can't steal.

I know that when it first happened,
I liked it.
I know that some nights
I can't forget the role
I had in my own dying.

and what do I know about salvation?

it's the missing feeling
it's my body suspended from the ceiling.
it's the thought
that I could one day
leave myself behind,

that I could save myself
from my own hands

from my own kind.

3am, I Dig Myself a Grave From My Bed

fall through
new arms,

still blue.

come home
to someone,
I want to come
home to you.

I am
diseased in the only place
I have ever felt love

a particular
warmth at the tip
of the gun.

I am
face down in
the dirt,

eyes gouged open,
overflowing
with
worms

crawl out of them.

my blood on the white parts
of your fingernails,

like nail polish but less feminine,
and not masculine,

not quite of this earth at all.

It's like I've offended God.

my blood is blasphemy

my tears are gall.

It is my ancestral stain
that is upon you all,
my profane red vein

rupture.

me upon
man.

me upon
you.

undiluted rapture.

girl bleeds
like a perpetual menstruation,

girl goes faster.

I crawl out of this dream
I call out of myself

give me real
give me real

spiral
into
uncertainty,
go ahead,
girl,

spin the wheel.

For Something So Lovely, Violence

sketched on
cereal boxes
and road signs,
a considerate disaster.

there is a general
disappointment
that stinks up the basement

and mother is dressed in superfluous
layers of pink
she tells me
what I need to hear

fake feminine sculptures
fall
babies who fail to learn
how to walk
crawl
and it's all porcelain pieces
on the ground at the end of the film

they dig into the skin of my foot
I see color again
I am new,
newly destroyed

I am powder under fingernails
and the alcohol that runs in your arteries
and the spilled drink
that made your friend slip and break his arm

and the lost insect that finds refuge
in your car's dashboard

this is all too violent
sometimes
for something so lovely
as life

only now have I forgotten
what to do

every year,
I tell myself something new

this year,
there is something in me that
knows not what it takes
but what it gives

I am open like a wound
at the surgeon's hand
palming away like a beggar
beg
beg
beg harder

the holy trinity
of being
giving
and needing

the holy trinity
of you

and me
and god
jammed in between us

like a knife in a stale loaf of bread

this is all too violent
sometimes
for something so lovely
as life

Dissociation of the Self

Novel Saturday evening
on the news.
You sing in my ear,
and I hum you the blues.
What else should we lose?
ourselves?

I put a timer on the rain,
like it won't ever come down
this way again.

I put a timer on our love,
two days, two weeks,
in the house of my body,
the ceiling leaks,

the floors are made of paper,
and it smells like smoke
and wasted potential.
The rain, too, breaks,

when we hold it too closely.

Dismal December,
it never comes without taking.

This time what will it take?

Truth is:
I am a distorted image
of expectation and reality,

of putting a time frame
on everything,
even my own life.

Truth is:
there is never enough truth.

Truth is:
you cannot own me
any more than I own myself,
which is not at all,
which is a conflict
of grasp and grasp
and name this
and name that

and sell myself
to the night,
and to the day,
and to you,
for whom I stay

In this prison I call skin.
But I am a walking contradiction,
I call it my sin,
living and dying

Like it's my duty
as a woman
to carve myself out:

Tear the ligaments

spare the breasts
rip the lips off
leave the paint
cut the legs off
leave the skirt
pull the head out
leave the hair.

This delusion is mine to bear,
and whoever cares enough to listen.

Poet says: *Is my blood artistic enough?*

Woman says: *Is my blood appropriate enough?*

Actress says: *Is my blood realistic enough?*

Truth is:
we don't know
a line exists
between sacrifice and love.

I time everything
because I can never sell myself enough
to make anyone stay.

I time the rain.

we try to hold it,
but it slips away.

Will it always be this way?

Resurrection in December

This first of December,
The trees dry themselves out,
The leaves fall and fall.
And how sweet the blood is
When it no longer fills

The vessel of my body.
Yet still I suffocate under
The razors — your lungs
Hidden behind contused skin.

And the gods would've
Condemned you,
Giver of impurity.
But one cannot grow

Into disgust
When one has only
Seen your tender touch,
Not the way in which

Your fingernails glisten
When coated in blood.
You are purebred,
Sick animal,

Your mother is no saint,
Your father lives burdened.
And how I suffocate in the act: inhale!
Exhale! and all things that
Come in between.

How unfair it is
To live and live
With the weight of your
Disease still trying to kill me.

O you have exhausted my very
Being, pulled at my limbs,
Stolen all my dreams
Like Lucifer himself.
(I no longer dream, I no longer dream!)

If this is where life ends,
then it is where death begins.
But I shall wake on the third of December!
A living unexpected.
A woman: resurrected.

Dead Man's Pose

It's the act I fear,
treading lightly over it,
making love to it
in the dark,
where my trembling
might resemble orgasming,
and where I might
not feel the shame of it all.

Stealthy like a thief
I walk with it,
cross paths with it
in some Van Gogh night,
the moon hanging down from the sky
like a silver earring,
like a chandelier,

When suddenly it pierces through my ear.
I was caught.

You can,
you cannot.

Morality is insanity,
Loving my mind is vanity
on your part
and surrender on mine.

And there is nothing else.

We are not gods,

not priests,
not sentenced to sermonize
or obey.
You are a predator--
I am your prey:

My back, your dinner table,
My heart, your poetry,
My face, the pillow
you rest your head upon.

My cause of death
is always asphyxiation,
always extremism,
always adoration.

It's the act I fear.

You tell me that I am at my best
when I am crying
or going through a lack of sleep
in fear of dying.

It's the act I fear:

Waking to find my life has passed me by,
that I've been sucked dry
by whatever these men mean,
by whatever it is that overcomes the
I, I, I, every time.

And as I walk under the moon,
the moon waves goodbye,

goodbye,
goodbye.

You fear the act,
you die--
you die.

You Have a Habit of Romanticizing the Dead

I dream of something
without a heart,
don't kiss me,
don't analyze me,
don't start.

I dream that I
am able to reach inside
and give birth
to myself,

something of a miracle,
no one knowing where
I came from,
no one knowing what
I'm made of.

I dream of something
without a heart.
I wish I could tell them
that hydrangeas are not hydrangeas
if they're dead,

They're no longer Chopin in the summer,
no longer red lips in the winter,
no longer every masochist's dream
and every child's ceremonial splinter.

Hydrangeas are not hydrangeas

if they're dead.

So if you see me laying in a field
somewhere,
the moon on my face,
the sun on my back,
don't carry me home.

My fate is my fate alone,
and I am more skin than I am bone,

My arms flail
like I can fly,
you kiss my head
with such pity,
like I were to die
tomorrow.

I dream about things
without a heart,
like when she screamed at me
from the balcony,
what is this, Romeo and Juliet?

She wiped the love off of her face
like sweat.
I wish I were a hydrangea
instead.

You thought that I could forget,
rosemary burning in the field,
my white tights are ruined
from kneeling in the dirt,

And kneeling
and kneeling.

What is this silence,
what is this feeling.
I wish for the things that
have no meaning:

the destruction of our youth,
the loveless moments we find ourselves in
bed with,
the fact that we're lasting longer
than our lives are.

I wish for the things that have no meaning,
like when you kissed me
and told me I was pretty
because I was a writer,

As if I looked like,
If someone walked past me,
my heart would break
and the lines would pour out of me,

as if I looked like a person at all,
with my fragments laid out on your
bedroom floor,
the fan moving slowly
like a clock's hands,
telling of the time
we have left,

which is none.

As if I looked like
I was moments
away from falling apart
and somehow
that was “pretty”
and not tragic
and not eternally
and utterly haunting.

And once again,
I dream of things
that cannot part,
something without a face,
something without a heart.

The Waiting Game

Follow the lines
On your arm.
Follow the roots,
my black
platform boots
in the dirt.

One, two, one.

Follow me
into the water,
into the rain,
into what feels good
and into what leaves you
in pain.

Follow me, insane,
back to where you first found me.

Poke at the life of me,
Slap it,
Watch my skin
Glow in lasting reds.

Two, three, four.

I wish I could touch again.
I wish I could feel ecstasy
and ache,

for in it

lies the hesitance:
buried within,
forgotten,
rediscovered.

In it lies the truth
behind my desperation,
my body
like glass
at the hand

of a knife.
And if a knife were a hand,
it would be yours.

I don't believe in the future;
it's not a poem worth writing.
and I don't believe in the past,

it's not a fate worth fighting
for.

I don't want tomorrow
I don't want to wait

I don't want to love you
I don't like to hate

And I hold his hand
but it's yours that remains

pierced right through me

What is left in the end
is always but a fragment,

but a string of photographs
thrown into a box and forgotten.

What is left in the end
is always the water,

the follow me,
follow me,
softer,
softer,

I don't want tomorrow,
But can it come faster.
Follow me
follow the laughter.

What Does It Mean?

Calling out for someone to pick up
And temperamental
Blue nights,
Your head on the bed,

My face on your mind,
Nothing, no one is too kind,
There is no such thing.

The phone does not ring.

You kiss my body
like you're scared
but of what?

You hand me a glass of water,
I hand you my heart,
Bloody, bitten into,
a dream, a memento,
a symbol.

Does it scare you
that nothing scares me?

I don't want to be civil.
Quit telling me
that there is order
in love
when it is clear
that there is none,

When I push you away
when I want you close.
Why do we cling
To that which hurts us the most,
Like art on a wall
On a nail

On the ground.

What is lost
Will never be found
The same in the end,

Like I will never be anyone's
Like I am yours,

Like you will see my face
Anywhere you end up,
whether you are miles away,

or the only thing
between us is a door.

My death,
I will flaunt it
Like a pretty dress,
Red and scorned,
and I am a whore.

My lady-like manners,
Gone and mourned.

Gone under the skin,

like dirt under a nail,
like your fingers in my hair,

Where do they go
when you don't show,
when the night is drenched
in melancholy

and your body
is not next to my body,

where are your fingers?
where is your heart?
was it love, in the end,
that tore us apart?

I am your girl,
I am your bitch,
I am yours
yours yours yours,

Changing all the I's
in my vocabulary to ours
feels like putting flowers
on a grave,

making it lovely
that we know nothing about one other
except that we want to touch
and possess
and cry when we can't
have sex.

What does it mean to you?

Well, it means more than I can say.

You go your way,
And I go mine,

Neither of us mind.

What does it mean to you?

It means a moment.
It means a rhyme,

It means you give me
a poem,
and I give you my time.

Half in the Light, Half in the Closet

She asks about hunger,
and I respond with eyes closed as,
like the coming down of rain,
the stage lights
come down on my face,

and I, a small child
like I once was,
stand in the closet of shame.
The closet where I find myself
time and time again,

where silence that breathes
down my neck
disentangles the
voice that I keep tucked away
somewhere in that child's body.

How do I tell
about desire?

How do I tell
about anything at all?

I stand like a child
in the nightmare
of my wants.
And my eyes
full of shooting stars

That are like ropes,

that shoot out of them.
that you pull, that you pull.
Oh how you pull, how you pull
your way into my soul—

And do I know about hunger?

Yes, I know.
I know about that
bullet in my stomach,
the one I keep there—
despite the wound,
despite everything else.

I know about my want of you.

Back to the Town

Back to the small town
Where the houses line up:
Cinder, wishful,
As they wait to be filled with life.

The birds almost blend in
With the rocks on the ground,
Cracked pieces of land all around.
And I sit,
And I watch.

There's a sweet little house
That stares at me,
Its blue door opens and closes
As the breeze comes and goes.

I think how passing the moment is,
How the wind is never really here,
Yet we feel it go,
And it leaves nothing behind.

Will we, too, leave nothing behind
When it's time for us to go?

We already tear into each other's lives,
Make almost nothing out of each other's souls.

Back to the small town
Where the beaches used to be empty
But are now full,
Are now raging with the beats

Of a million hearts.

Back to the small town,
Perpetual but ever changing.
Always here,
Not forever.

Will we, too, leave nothing behind?

Transaction

Unlearn my every vowel,
Speak in a stare,
Speak in a howl,

They say sex is sold
More than it is bought.

They say I'm on sale today,
And the price is unspoken:

What are you willing to pay
For something that's broken?

A whisper,
A handshake,
A girl underneath her own bed,
Both the frightened and the frightening.

Girl is the persecuted
And the executioner.

I'll die by my own hand
And call it oneness.

I'll burn myself
Like a witch at the stake,
Like I have more truth to tell
Than this world can take.

World-ending
Orgasmic deaths

And soul transactions.
It aches more than you know.

Acid, vodka, blow,
The jeans tear,
The eyes tear,
My left ear,
My right ear,

I am imbued with fear.
Are you afraid?

Sell me like cheap liquor.

They say sex is sold
More than it is bought.

I say I sell myself
More than I breathe.
I say I lose myself
Like losing teeth.

One by one,
Coldly, wholly,
Like killing myself,
Like dying slowly.

Like I am dying
Slowly.

A Wish By The Stream

For F.

I was down by the stream
This afternoon,
And I came across a light.
It glided on the water,
It sparkled and gleamed.
It shot my eyes
Only a glance
Before it went away.

And that's only to say
And not to say
That I came across you
This afternoon.
A reflection in the blue
And the green,
And even the bee
That sat on my arm,
Yellow and black,
For a minute or two

Before it took me
Back to you.
And that's only to say
That you showed
Yourself again to me
For the millionth
Time this week,
This month,
This half-year.

You fade out of the
Heaviness of life
When it comes to living
It with me,
But you're still
The only thing I see.

I saw you this afternoon,
And that's not to say
You were really there,
Just that I saw you.
You looked the same,
With leaves on the
Hedges of your forehead,
With clouds in your eyes.
And water on your cheeks,
The bluest I've ever seen.

You held my hand
After I tripped over what
I later discovered only a pebble.
Life is never that harsh,
You whispered.
And it never was.

You sang to me so softly
After my encounter
With the tombs on the other side
Of the stream.
You sang yourself so softly,
Undressed death,
Called me to your heart
Like you had once

When life was much simpler
Than it is now.

You loved of me so much
That I could not believe
Anything of pain,
Even the leaves fell
On my cheek like rain.
Nothing could touch me
But you,
And that was not new.

Now the stream
I visited this afternoon,
I heard,
Only ever speaks of you,
(Like I do, like I do)
And the wind blows away the hair
From my stone face,
And promises me
There is a place.
A place where you still beat on,
Stubborn and steady,
On and on.

A place where you still love me,
Where you still love.
Where the skies only speak of miracles
While they rest above.
They say,
Life is never that harsh.

Now listen to me,

I was down by the stream
This afternoon,
And I came across you.
This is not to say we finally touched,
Just that this time I wished it enough.

Smoke Break

Keep your apron on,
We won't be here too long
Cigarette hanging off your lip,
Sweat on your eyebrow,
I've always seen people
As something to lose
Rather than to gain.

It's not morning,
It's not night,
It's all the same.

We cast shadows as insignificant
as those of insects
that crawl away on the ground
as they wait to be stomped out
into oblivion.

Do you believe that you're God?

I think the smoke
Gives me wings,
And if I dream long enough,
Ignore my alarm long enough,
I might fly away.

And who am I to stay?

And who are you?

I've always seen people as things to lose

Rather than to gain
And I'm late for it all again.

I've felt like an awkward guest
My entire life,
One foot in their door,
The other in yours,
Tense like I'll be stoned
if I'm not let in.

I used to say living was my sin,
Like looking in the mirror
Like picking at the skin
Like I don't know when that movie ends
or when it begins

and I've got my body stretched out
on the floor
ready
with my eyes towards the television,

I'm a trembling star,
I know it.

I like how the lights feel on my face
when I'm alone,
or when I'm in front of
an audience

I like how it feels
to feel like someone is watching.
One foot in their door,
the other in yours.

We've got to show up at dawn
when they open the doors
if we want to catch life
while it's still here.

Keep your apron on,
The roof burns on our bare feet,
It's summer again.
Why am I pretending I am someone
I am not?

I dream of underground bar blues,
I look at you,
and you kiss my bruise
And tell me not to fall again.

I won't.
I don't have wings.
I don't have things.

All I have is a dream
and some change,
the movement, the ache,
and this moment of
catching life during
a smoke break.

Otra Parte De Ti

Ven acércate mas a mi
Dame mas que tu piel,
Otra parte de ti.

La respiracion.
El momento.

Yo te espero,

Ahi adonde la oscuridad
Se mezcla con el tiempo,
escribiendo estrellas en un cielo
que no esta.

Pidiendo libertad
lejos de lo que tengo
que me quiere consumir,

lo quemo,
pero
sigue caminando
Y sin mi.

Todavia llegare, llegare,
me encontrare en

esa parte de ti.

Canta y no llores
Canta para que no llores

Sobran los dolores
Sobran los dias

Sobra eso y esto
Y todo lo que es
Yo te hablo en español
Y tu me hables en ingles

Y no hay idioma que nos detenga
No hace falta que me comprendas
a mi

Yo existo en otro mundo
En otro idioma
En la ocuridad,

En esa parte de ti.

The Seasons Away From Home

The coming of spring,
The wait for the fall,
When you get home,
Won't you tell them I love them all?

All the seasons
In that country,
All the people there I miss,
And the mouth,
The mouth I did not kiss.

I've been in my own head
Far too often,
Where I let time pass
While I think of everything
I could have but don't.

Tell her I love her
How I wrote all that time ago,
For the berries hold on again
To the bushes on which they grow,
And soon, I will be home.

The loneliness does not last a lifetime,
Or so I hope,
As I put in your palm a few poems
I wrote on the kitchen floor
And never gave to her,
To whom I wrote them for.

We used to be so close

That even the sheets between us
Seemed to float above our bodies,
Hesitant to keep us apart.

But I had to go.
Now I'm in my head so often,
Almost all the time.
I drift off in conversation with others
To the one between us in my head.

I search every drawer,
Look out every window,
Stare in the mirror
And try to find her.

I will be home soon.
It will be time soon.
But during this coming of the spring,
While I wait for the fall,
When you get home,
Please tell them I love them all.

The tourists in the corner of every street,
The cars and the stars too big for the sky,
My love at the house from nine to five,
Always in search for more,
Always waiting for me.

Tell them, tell whoever,
That I'll be missing them forever.

The Darkest Night (I Was Fourteen)

The first night I spent there
I remember as the darkest night of the year.
I could hardly grasp the idea of living.
I reached out for my little sister's hand
And imagined her in the bed we used to share.
I used to think she didn't care.

But when I was let out, she told me she had cried
Thinking about me.

I thought, my mother dyes her hair blonde,
So she can look less like me
And more like herself.
Good for her.

I thought, my father walks in and out of my life
Like it is a revolving door,
And he has a job to do
That he can never stay at long enough
To finish.
Good for him.

I thought, men hate how I dress.
They think I should show more skin,
So I show more skin.
Am I good enough for him?

I thought, I leave myself undone too often,
Like another poem of mine.
But this is not poetry,
This is my life.

Is my life good enough for poetry?

Good. Good. Good.
I thought, I am over it.
Good exists,
But perhaps I am not good.
Perhaps I was born as one of those people
Made to give balance to the world,
Bad, so everyone else can be good.

I thought, I know that I have to do this for them,
I have been doing it for them since the first time
I thought about it:
The faces of my family
As they whisper the words to Our Father,
Their Catholic attempt to save me,
The blood at the end,
The attempt to mend
All that I have broken.

I have done it for them.

The first night I spent there
I remember as the darkest night of the year.
It felt like tears were the only proof
Of my life.

I had gone under it for hours,
The knife,
They examined me
Like dust under a microscope,
Asked me how I did it
Why I did it

When I did it.

I wanted to die,
I answered.

They shook their heads
Like they understood.
The first night was the darkest.
I promised I'd be good.

I Do Fill

Place right hand on left breast
and feel the heartbeat.
Feel the most precious pulsation:
how the heart beats and beats
its own life into being.
Someone has to do it,

And the sparks of yesterday have gone.
The crowds have dissolved into the
thick air of train stations.
Not even the railroads could keep
them grounded,

They came and went,
came and went.
They come and go.
I once touched a man,
Our shoulders brushed
against each other —

Bitter friction of death.
he went, he left.
I thanked the train stations
that night,
as he dissolved into
their thick airs.

I once touched a woman,
our touch almost real.
but more real were
the winds of disbelief

that two women —
countries apart

could ever learn to
l love and love again,
arms stretched out
over the miles ahead.
And the soul, the soul —
it goes,
it goes,
in with the already under the dirt.
In with the suffocated insects
that breathe death into the
lungs,

do not touch me!
I do not repose,
I decompose, I decompose.
place right hand on left breast
and feel the heartbeat!

It goes, it goes —
it pumps life into the soul.
Someone has to do it,
why not let it be yourself?

I sink into the dirt.
it does fill what
love no longer can.

I do fill what love no longer can.

Confession

For A.

is it cold?

have you come to the doorstep
with nothing left unshared,

with no fabric over your chest:
your heart exposed, but not despaired.

with your legs uncrossed,
telling of something that can't be found
where it has been lost.

when you were young,
you must have seen the blood first
before the wound.

you must have expected it:
for the leak to start beneath your skin,
the stagnation once it reached the vein.

(all artists steal from the rain)

whose is this?
is it mine?

I don't own it, you have said,

except you will
with time.

except you do this time.

is it cold?

have you come with
nothing silver on,
nothing gold?
perfect in the image of Yourself
you are.

primordial,
corporeal
peace.

Is it cold?

you have shivered;
it has brought me to my knees.

Mornings on the Other Side

For J.

We wake up at six every morning,
the cemetery bell rings.
And it smells like mourning
when you tell me about the dream you had
where I was a trapeze artist,

and you were the rope beneath me.

Does that mean that I hurt you?
I ask.

No, it means that we hurt each other,
you say,
and we welcome the day.

I take the head on my chest,
and I make a line out of it.

I take the shut eyes,
the light that peers through the shutters,
wanting a glimpse of us lovers.

the routine of it all,
and the madness.

I make a line out of it.

I tell you that I used to drink coffee every morning,
until I learned that it made me
feel like God,

and then it made me want to dissolve
into the blue walls of my bedroom,

so now I drink my coffee with milk.

In that way,
I mean to say,
change does not have to come
in extremes.

We change every morning.

I know you don't think
that anyone notices,
but poets notice everything.

We change every morning.

You, with your symbolic,
painful dreams,
eyes shut in the morning light,
and your lack of order
in everything
except love.

Me, with my coffee,
my lack of sleep
that I blame on you,
and my order in
everything
except love.

We wake up at six every morning.
The cemetery bell rings.

If I am the trapeze artist,
Does that mean I am above you?
I ask.

No, in my dream, you were walking on me,
but somehow I was above you,
you said.

Does that mean that you think you're better than me?

No. It means that I don't think either of us are better.
You walk the rope, I am it.
Neither of us are saints.

We wake up at six every morning.
The cemetery bell rings.
And we know everything today:
the dream, the love, the coffee.

A Story About Devotion

For Beli.

Let us treat commotion
As a sign of devotion.
The squirrel walks on a wire
Even in its sleep.
A lifetime, it seems,
It's spent with the same routine,
Not without a fall or two,
Not without a life or two.

And I own a tree,
(Excuse the possession,
As devotion is not always possession,
And I own only my soul).
The tree wavers in the wind,
And it carries the nests of birds
Long gone.

The nests don't allow space
For the tree's leaves,
But what shall the tree do?

And I sit here,
And I watch you,
My vision of centuries,
My sight more precious
Than time.
You point at the devotion outside,
And I am devoted to you,
My giver in blue.

Tell me a story,
If it breaks my heart,
I'll laugh it off.
Tell me a story,
I don't want to forget you.

And let's remember that love
Can translate to devotion,
And devotion to love.
When you disappear,
I will still be here.

And I'm always afraid,
And I always speak the wrong words,
But you still put me on your lap
And guide me with your voice,
If only in a dream.

Tell me a story
About devotion,
If it breaks my heart,
I would've expected it to.

S. Bruzon is a Cuban-American maker and curator of many kinds of art. Musician, actor, filmmaker, writer- she finds it impossible to limit herself to one medium of creative expression.

Reminiscent of the Confessional Poets that she loves best, her written work is an ocean of self-examination. Within her poetry, she rides waves of personal revelation, detailing every person, place, or moment that has ever marked her heart. In her debut collection, she hopes she has come to the page as open-minded and open-hearted as possible so that through her truth, someone else may find their own.

RELEASED BY DARK THIRTY POETRY

www.ingramcontent.com/pod-product-compliance
Lightning Source LLC
LaVergne TN
LVHW010110170826
845678LV00012B/2331

9781739254650